ROOTED REFLECTIONS

Rooted Reflections

Brittanie McQueen

Spireorbit
PUBLISHING

Contents

Rooted Reflections

A Companion to The Rooted Path
This workbook belongs to:

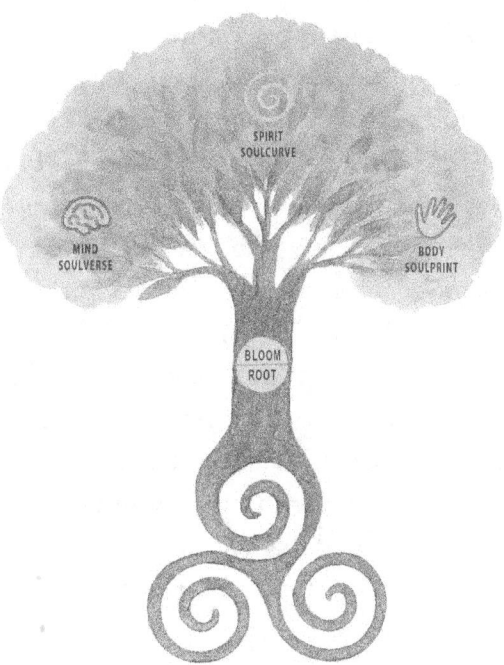

By Brittanie McQueen
Spireorbit Publishing
Greenwood, IN

Book design, cover image, illustrations and layout by Brittanie McQueen

Disclaimer & Scope of Practice

Brittanie is a trauma-informed guide and student of Ayurveda, holistic healing, and creative/spiritual practices. She holds certifications in trauma-informed care and other non-licensed fields of study. Her work is intended for education, reflection, and personal growth. She is **not a licensed medical, mental health, or crisis professional**, and her offerings are **not a substitute for professional care**. She does not diagnose, treat, or prescribe. Always seek the guidance of a qualified provider for any medical or mental health concerns.

This book is for educational purposes only. It is **not intended to replace professional medical, psychological, or therapeutic advice**. The following examples are fictional and are meant to illustrate how the Rooted Path may look in different situations. While they are inspired by real patterns and experiences, the details have been changed or created for clarity.

Trigger Warning: This book explores themes of trauma, healing, and emotional intensity. Some passages may bring old memories, sensations, or unresolved experiences to the surface. Please move at your own pace. Take breaks when needed. If the content becomes overwhelming, pause and return only when you feel ready. You are not alone.

Healing is nonlinear. You are sovereign in how you walk this path. If you need immediate support, please reach out to a licensed therapist, medical provider, or crisis care resource in your area. Take what resonates. Leave what does not. Honor your well-being first, always.

For permissions, licensing inquiries, or training in The Rooted Path method, please contact:
ecoboundearth@gmail.com
www.ecoboundholistics.com

Welcome & How to Use This Workbook

The Rooted Path is a guide to transforming stress, anxiety, and emotional triggers into steadiness, clarity, and growth.

When old wounds resurface or daily stress builds, most of us fall into two familiar patterns, pushing our feelings down or letting them spill out. Neither brings lasting peace. What if there were another way that honored your body, your energy, and your spirit?

Drawing from modern neuroscience, ancient healing traditions, and lived experience, Brittanie McQueen introduces The Rooted Path, a practical framework anyone can use in the moment a trigger arises. Through clear steps and grounding practices, you'll learn how to activate awareness of your body's signals before they take over. Transmute emotional energy into strength through simple breath, imagery, and elemental practices. Integrate calm and clarity so your body knows the moment is truly over. Embody resilience in daily life, at work, in relationships, in parenting, and within yourself.

Whether you're carrying stress, grief, or anxiety, or simply longing for a steadier way of living, The Rooted Path offers tools you can return to again and again.

This workbook is a companion to The Rooted Path: A Gentle Return to Wholeness and is intended for you to use at your own pace. You may find that you skip around, spiral back, free write, doodle, and take breaks at any time. Let yourself get into a creative flow.

1

The Rooted Path & Tree of Becoming

The Tree of Becoming is a living image of your wholeness. Each part of the tree reflects a part of you, reminding you that growth is both steady and alive.

Roots – Steadiness & Grounding

Roots are the unseen anchors of your life. They hold your history, your patterns, your deep belonging to the earth. To tend your roots is to remember what steadies you and to gently notice what keeps you stuck.

Trunk – Awakening the Spirit Within

The trunk is your inner self strong, steady, always growing upward. It represents the awakening of your spirit within you, the core of who you are becoming. The trunk carries life from the roots into every other part of the tree.

Branches – Mind, Body, Spirit Alignment

The branches reach outward, connecting you with the world. They represent the harmony of mind, body, and spirit working together. When your branches are healthy, you feel balanced and aligned in every area of life.

Fruit – Joy & Passion

The fruit is what your life offers to you and to others. It is your joy, your passions, your creative energy, the nourishment that flows naturally when you are rooted, awake, and aligned. Fruit is not forced; it ripens as you grow.

Guided Meditation: The Tree of Becoming

Find a comfortable place to sit or stand. Close your eyes and take a slow, deep breath in. Let it out gently, feeling your body begin to soften.

Roots

Imagine roots extending from the soles of your feet deep into the earth. Feel them growing downward, steady and strong, anchoring you to the ground beneath you. With every breath, your roots sink deeper, carrying away tension and drawing in nourishment. Whisper to yourself: "I am grounded. I am steady."

Trunk

Now bring your attention to the center of your body, your spine, your core. See yourself as the trunk of the tree: upright, alive, awake. Your spirit flows here, connecting earth to sky, inner self to outer life. Whisper: "I am awake. I am whole within."

Branches

Let your awareness rise through your chest, your shoulders, your arms. See your branches reaching outward in every direction, mind, body, and spirit extending into harmony. Your branches stretch toward light, toward connection, toward balance. Whisper: "I am aligned in mind, body, and spirit."

Fruit

Finally, imagine blossoms appearing on your branches, slowly ripening into fruit. These fruits are your joy, your passions, your gifts, what nourishes you and others. See them shining, vibrant, abundant, ready to be shared. Whisper: "I am alive with joy. My life nourishes myself and others."

Take a final deep breath, feeling the whole tree within you. Roots grounding you, trunk awakening you, branches aligning you, fruit bringing joy. When you are ready, open your eyes, carrying this steadiness and aliveness into your day.

Healing and Growth

The Tree of Becoming reminds us that healing and growth are not separate from joy. As you tend your roots, awaken your trunk, and align your branches, you naturally begin to bear fruit. You cultivate a life that is steady, alive, and nourishing to yourself and others.

When we cling too tightly to a specific outcome or to how we think it should arrive, we actually cut ourselves off from the many ways it could arrive. Life often delivers in ways more creative, surprising, and generous than we could have imagined.

In these moments it can mean that you are meant to soften your grip. Surrender here doesn't mean giving up. It means softening your grip, letting the flow carry you instead of bracing against it. Surrender isn't just about letting go of fear or control. It's also about leaning fully into what lights you up.

Don't hold yourself back from what makes you come alive. That's the most natural magnetism there is. Joy and passion are currents that carry you closer to your true self. When you're absorbed in creating, writing, making art, helping others that's when your energy becomes magnetic. People feel it. Opportunities find you. The "flow" moves easier because you're aligned with what naturally gives you life.

Instead of asking "When will this happen? How will it happen?" ask "Who am I being as I wait, as I create, as I walk this path?" Because who you are being is the real magnet. If you're rooted, alive in your passions, open to joy, the outcomes naturally line up.

This is exactly like the Tree of Becoming. You don't force fruit to appear. You tend the roots, steady the trunk, align the branches. The fruit ripens because of who the tree is being, not because it demanded a certain outcome.

The Breath of Surrender

1. Inhale — Breathe in through your nose, imagining you're gathering all the tension, worries, and gripping. "I gather what I've been holding."
2. Pause — Hold the breath gently for 2 counts. "I acknowledge it is here."
3. Exhale — Release slowly through your mouth, imagining it all softening into the earth or into open hands that can hold more than you. "I surrender this. I am held."

A Surrender Mantra

Here's a simple Surrender-to-Being Mantra you can carry with you. This keeps you rooted in presence, while reminding you that outcomes are natural results, not something you have to chase.

"I release the outcome. I tend to who I am becoming. The fruit will ripen in its time."

In the next section we are going to look at your roots. What is holding you now and how to become more steady and grounded.

Naming your roots

The Rooted Path focuses on your roots and creating a steady foundation. This will become your new baseline of living. You may still slip at times but if you notice and reroute yourself, you will not slip fully back into old routines.

Our roots are the patterns, stories, and experiences that shape us. Some roots steady us and give us strength, while others keep us tangled or stuck. Healing begins with noticing what is underneath the surface — not to judge or rip it all out, but to listen. When we can name our roots, we start to see which ones nourish us and which ones we may need to release or transform. This is the first step of becoming: remembering that what lies beneath us matters.

Start by naming the gentle roots. These are small triggers that pull at you in daily life. Gentle roots are easiest to work with before tackling deeper roots. After naming your gentle roots, name your deeper roots. These may be trauma based, depression, deep fears and anxieties.

Our roots are the patterns and experiences that anchor us. Some roots steady us, while others keep us stuck. Naming them is the first step toward healing and becoming. We are not working with the deep roots yet. We are only naming them so we acknowledge what they are. Once you have written those down, take a moment to breathe with me. Take a deep breath in, hold, and release. Do this a few times until you feel more calm.

Gentle Roots	**Deep Roots**

Gentle Roots	Deep Roots

Journaling Prompts

If my life were a tree, what would my roots look like right now?

Where in my life do I already feel rooted and steady?

Where do I feel ungrounded or uncertain about who I am becoming?

What would it mean for you to be more rooted?

What aspects of your life might benefit from living with more steady roots?

What are three challenges that you would like to overcome?

If there were no limitations on who you could be, who are you becoming?

What daily practices (breath, movement, prayer, writing) help me feel connected to mind, body, and spirit?

Creative Prompt

Draw or collage your "root system." Include the people, practices, and places that nourish you, and also the tangled roots that may hold you back.

Root Reflections
(doodles or notes from my path)

Root Reflections
(doodles or notes from my path)

2

Rooted Choices

Affirmation: *"I am not limited to either/or. I step back, breathe, and see new paths. From my roots, I choose with confidence."*

When we are unrooted, decisions often feel urgent and narrow. It can seem like there are only two paths: yes or no, stay or go, right or wrong. But when we pause to ground ourselves, we realize there are often more possibilities. Roots give us the steadiness to step back, breathe, and notice options we couldn't see before. Being rooted allows us to choose from confidence, not fear.

Guided Practice

1. Write down the decision or situation that feels heavy or pressing.

2. Name the two "obvious" choices in front of you.

3. Place your hand on your heart, take three slow breaths.
4. Whisper: "I allow more to be possible."
5. Step back in your imagination and ask: "What other paths might be here?"
6. Write down any new possibilities, even if they seem small, creative, or unexpected.

Journaling Prompts

What decision feels most alive for me right now?

What are the two obvious choices I see?

How does my body respond when I imagine each choice?

If I step back, what other options become visible?

Which path feels most aligned with my rooted, steady self?

How would it feel to choose from fear? How would it feel to choose from steadiness?

Creative Prompt

Draw a simple tree with roots and branches. Write the "obvious" choices in the lower branches. Then add new branches for the hidden paths you discovered.

Rooted Choice Reflections
(doodles or notes)

3

Powerful Tools for Your Path

On my own journey and through the resources I share on my website, I've found certain categories of tools to be especially powerful. These are not just methods I've studied, they're living practices I've used and seen work for others. You can explore them as-is or adapt them into your own language and rhythm.

Ayurveda — Ayurveda offers grounding rituals tailored to your constitution and current state. Whether it's sipping warm spiced tea for comfort, doing self-massage with warm oil, or adjusting your daily rhythm to match the sun, these practices help your body feel safe enough to shift energy.

Herbalism — Plants carry their own energy and medicine. Chamomile to soften tension, tulsi for uplifting, lemon balm for soothing the heart, these are not just physical remedies, but allies for your emotional state. Herbal teas, tinctures, and even the act of brewing can become part of your ritual.

Crystals — Stones act as physical anchors. Black tourmaline for protection, rose quartz for self-compassion, clear quartz for clarity, each can serve as a touchstone in moments of activation. Holding them in your hand gives your body something to focus on as you work with the charge.

Sound — Sound moves energy. It can be as simple as humming, playing a singing bowl, or listening to a song that shifts your state. The vibration bypasses the thinking mind and works directly with the body's rhythm.

Mantra — A few words, spoken with intention, can be a life-line. "I am safe." "I return to center." "I choose peace." Choose phrases that feel true in your bones, not just your mind.

Meditation — Meditation doesn't have to mean sitting still for hours. Even two minutes of mindful breathing, or placing awareness on a single sensation, can be enough to keep you on the path when a charge rises.

Breath — Your breath is always with you and it is one of the fastest ways to influence your nervous system. Slow exhales, box breathing, or simply pausing to notice the breath can create the
space you need to respond instead of react.

Creativity — Drawing, painting, writing, singing, creative acts give energy a place to go. They don't have to be "good" to be effective. They just have to be honest.

Movement — Walking, stretching, yoga, dancing, shaking, movement helps energy complete its cycle. Even subtle shifts, like rolling your shoulders or swaying in your seat, can release tension.

Writing — Journaling can help you name the charge without drowning in it. Sometimes the act of putting words on paper is enough to loosen energy's grip.

Nature — The natural world is a master of regulation. Standing barefoot on the earth, listening to water, watching clouds move, nature invites your body back into its own rhythm.

Connection — We are wired for resonance. Talking to someone who can hold space without judgment, sitting in the presence of a calm friend, or even placing a hand on your own heart with compassion, these are all forms of connection that bring us back to center.

How to Build Your Toolkit

Start with what works now. Make a list of things that already help you feel more steady, even in small ways.

Choose one tool from each sense. Something to touch, something to hear, something to smell, something to see, something to move with.

Create a portable version. A small bag or pouch with a stone, a tiny vial of essential oil, a folded piece of paper with your mantra, and earbuds for music. Practice before you need it.

Don't wait for a crisis to try your tools. Use them when you're calm so your body associates them with safety.

Evolve as you grow. Some tools will fade. Others will deepen. Your toolkit should change as you do.

4

The Fog and the Call

"When the fog rolls in, it asks you to slow down and listen.
   Somewhere beyond the mist, a voice is calling you home."

The fog shows up when life feels muted or blurred, when we are going through the motions but not truly alive. It can feel heavy, even endless and yet the fog is also an invitation. Within it, a whisper begins to rise: there must be more than this. That whisper is the call. The call may stir restlessness or longing, but it is a sign that you are waking up. Both the fog and the call are thresholds that ask you to pause, the other invites you to step forward. Together, they prepare you for the journey into deeper clarity.

In this section we will focus on naming where you have felt foggy and where you have felt the call. Write down when you remember feeling like you are under the fog. And then write down times that you have felt a stirring or restlessness through the fog. The fog can feel heavy, but it is also an invitation. The call comes to remind us that the fog is not the end, it is the threshold to a new way of living.

The Fog	The Call

The Fog   **The Call**

Journaling Prompts

Where do I feel 'foggy' in my life right now?

What small whispers or calls have been tugging at me?

What do I feel called to do in this life that I am not currently doing?

What small changes could I make today towards my calling?

Creative Prompt

Write a short poem or freewrite beginning with: "When the fog surrounds me, I..." Then write another beginning with: "When the call comes, I..." Notice the shift between them.

The Fog & Call Reflections
(doodles or notes)

5

Noticing the Pulse

Affirmation: *I notice the signals of my body and trust them to guide me.*
Beneath the surface of our thoughts, the body is always speaking. A quickened heart-beat, a knot in the stomach, a rush of heat. These are not accidents, but signals. The pulse is the language of our nervous system, letting us know when we feel safe and when we are threatened. Learning to notice the pulse is learning to listen to your body's truth. It is not about controlling or silencing your sensations, but about honoring them as guides on your path to steadiness.

Grounding Before You Begin
Before you start writing, take a moment to ground yourself. Place your hand over your heart and your other hand on your belly. Close your eyes and take three slow breaths. Feel your chest and stomach rise and fall. Whisper to yourself: "I am safe to notice. I am safe to listen. I am safe to be here." When you feel ready, open your eyes and gently begin your journaling.

Where do I feel my emotions?	**What does it feel like?**

Where do I feel my emotions?	What does it feel like?

Journaling Prompts

When I feel stressed or unsettled, where do I notice it first in my body?

What sensations do I often ignore or push past?

Can I recall a time when my body warned me before my mind caught up?

What did that feel like?

What sensations in my body feel like "yes"? What sensations feel like "no"?

When do I notice my heartbeat most clearly? What does it remind me of?

What small signals tell me I am safe and steady?

Creative Prompt
Trace the outline of a body (you can use a simple figure sketch). Mark with colors, symbols, or words where you most often feel your pulse or sensations.

Noticing the Pulse Reflections
(doodles or notes)

6

Activate

Affirmation: *I have tools within me to shift my state and return to balance.*
When a trigger rises, it can feel as though the moment has taken over. Yet within you are simple, powerful tools that can activate a shift; breath, movement, grounding, imagery. To activate is to choose presence over autopilot. It is the moment you say, I will not be swept away by this storm. I will return to myself. Each practice you learn here is a way to steady your nervous system and remind your body that it is safe.

Guided Practice
1. Notice the Charge

Pause when you feel energy rising. Ask yourself:

Where do I feel this most in my body?

What does it feel like (tight, hot, buzzing, heavy)?

2. Stay Present

Instead of pushing it away, bring gentle awareness to the sensation.

Place a hand over the area of your body where you feel it most.

Take three slow breaths, imagining your breath flowing into that space.

3. Describe, Don't Judge

Write a few words or whisper them to yourself:

"This feels like fire in my chest."

"This feels like pressure in my throat."

Let description replace judgment.

4. Support the Holding

If the charge feels strong, add a support:

Breathe out longer than you breathe in.

Repeat a mantra: "I can hold this. I am safe."

Touch something grounding (a stone, the floor, your own hands).

5. Release Gently

After a few moments, notice if the intensity shifts. It may soften, move, or stay the same. Either way, you have practiced presence. Close by whispering: "I stayed with it. I am steady. I can hold my charge."

Tracking Activation

Situation / Trigger	First Sensation I Noticed	Tool I Used

Reflection

How It Felt After	What I Learned

Tracking Activation

Situation / Trigger	First Sensation I Noticed	Tool I Used

Reflection

How It Felt After	What I Learned

Activate Journal Prompts

When I feel a charge rise, what does it feel like in my body?

How long can I stay with the sensation before I feel the urge to push it away or act on it?

What thoughts or fears come up when I try to sit with the charge?

How does my body know the difference between holding with presence and holding with tension?

What helps me remember that the charge will pass if I stay present with it?

What small practices (breath, touch, mantra) support me in holding rather than reacting?

After holding with a charge, how do I feel afterward compared to when I avoid or numb it?

Creative Prompt

Create a "charge symbol." Use shapes, lines, or colors to represent what a charge feels like in your body. Then, beside it, draw or write the tools you reach for to help you hold with it.

Activation Reflections
(doodles or notes)

7

Transmutation

Affirmation: *I can transform what overwhelms me into strength and wisdom.*
Energy cannot be destroyed, but it can be changed. The emotions that rise within us like fear, anger, grief which are not here to punish us. They are energy moving through. To transmute is to take what feels heavy and allow it to become light, to shift what once felt unbearable into something usable. Through imagination, breath, and intentional focus, you can change the shape of your experience, turning pain into strength and agitation into clarity.

Guided Practice

Find a quiet space and close your eyes.

Take a slow breath in… and a long, steady breath out.

1. Sense the Energy

Bring your awareness to the feeling that feels heavy, tight, or overwhelming.

Notice where it lives in your body.

2. Give it a Form

Imagine this energy taking shape.

Is it a stone? A storm cloud? A tangled knot?

Let it appear however it wants — no right or wrong.

3. Breathe Into It

With each inhale, imagine your breath surrounding the shape.

With each exhale, imagine it softening, loosening, or shifting.

4. Watch it Transform

See the shape begin to change:

A stone growing lighter, turning into sand that flows away.

A dark cloud thinning into soft mist and lifting.

A knot loosening, strand by strand, until it is free.

5. Receive the New Form

Notice what has emerged in place of the heaviness.

Does it feel lighter? Warmer? More open?

Whisper to yourself:

"I allow what feels heavy to change. I receive its new form."

Take one more deep breath, gently open your eyes, and write what you experienced.

Tracking Transmutation

The Energy I Felt	How It Appeared to Me

Reflection

The Transformation	What I Learned

The Energy I Felt	How It Appeared to Me

Reflection

The Transformation	What I Learned

What emotions or energies feel the heaviest for me right now?

If I gave this feeling a shape, color, or texture, what would it look like?

How does this energy move in my body (tight, buzzing, frozen, swirling)?

What would it look or feel like if this energy softened, melted, or shifted form?

I magine this energy as an ally — what wisdom might it be carrying for me?

How has my pain or struggle in the past ever transformed into strength, compassion, or clarity?

If I could rewrite the story of this energy, what would it become?

Creative Prompt

Choose a heavy emotion you carry. Write it in big letters across the page. Then, beneath it, rewrite or redraw it transformed, a new word, new image, new color that it becomes when shifted.

Transmutation Reflections
(doodles or notes)

8

Integrate

Affirmation: *I welcome calm and clarity into my whole being.*

When a charge softens or shifts, your body may still hold echoes of tension. Integration is the step of gently telling your whole system: "It is over. I am safe now." This seals the work you've done so it doesn't unravel, and it invites your nervous system to return fully to peace. Integration is not about erasing what happened. It's about helping your body settle so you can carry forward steadiness.

Guided Practice

1. Sit comfortably and place your feet on the ground.

2. Rest one hand on your heart and the other on your belly.

3. Take a slow inhale… and an even slower exhale.

4. Whisper softly: "It is over. I am safe now."

5. Imagine a gentle wave of calm moving from your head down to your toes, releasing any lingering tension.

6. Stay for a few breaths, letting calm soak in.

Integrate Journaling Prompts

What situation or feeling am I choosing to settle into peace?

How can I tell when my body has truly relaxed?

What helps me remember that the moment has passed and I am safe?

Small rituals that help me carry peace into daily life (tea, walking, journaling, music, etc.):

Who or what in my life helps me feel most calm and regulated?

If I created a "peace anchor" (an object, word, or gesture), what would it be?

Creative Prompt

Design a ritual of calm. Sketch or describe the objects, actions, or settings that help you feel fully settled (a candle, a cup of tea, a walk, a phrase). Make it your own "integration altar" on paper.

Integration Reflections
(doodles or notes)

9

Embody

Affirmation: *I live from my rooted, steady self every day.*

Embodying is where the path becomes a way of life. It is no longer something you reach for only in moments of struggle. It becomes the steady rhythm you carry into ordinary days. Embodying does not mean being perfect. It means returning again and again to the practices, tools, and truths that root you. Each small choice to pause, to breathe, to notice, is embodiment. Over time, these choices weave into who you are, until steadiness is simply your way of being.

Guided Practice

1. Sit quietly and bring to mind the image of the Tree of Becoming.

2. See your roots steady, your trunk strong, your branches balanced, your fruit alive with joy.

3. Place both hands over your heart and whisper: "This is who I am."

4. Imagine yourself moving through your day (walking, speaking, creating, resting) with this same rooted steadiness.

5. Take three breaths, anchoring the image into your body.

Embody Journaling Prompts

Write a short statement that captures who you are becoming, in the present tense:

What simple daily actions help me live from steadiness?

How do I speak, move, and create when I am rooted and steady?

What relationships or situations already reflect the steadiness I'm cultivating?

What fears or doubts still rise when I imagine living fully as my embodied self?

How can I tell I am embodying growth in my life already?

What passions or joys feel most alive when I am grounded and whole?

Creative Prompt

Draw or design a symbol that represents your embodied self, a tree, a spiral, a word, or a shape that feels true.

Embody Reflections
(doodles or notes)

10

Final Closing Reflection

You have walked the Rooted Path through reflection, practice, and courage. Each page you have touched is part of your becoming. Take a moment now to pause. Breathe deeply. Place your hand over your heart. Notice how far you have come, and honor the roots you have tended along the way. This is not the end. It is a beginning. The path you have practiced here is one you can return to again and again, whenever life feels heavy or unclear.

Completion Ritual:

Write one word that describes how you feel in this moment.

Write one truth you want to carry forward.

Create a simple affirmation that feels alive in your body today. Example: "I am steady. I trust my path. I am becoming." Let these words be your companion as you continue into your daily life. You are rooted. You are becoming. You are whole.

www.ingramcontent.com/pod-product-compliance
Lightning Source LLC
Chambersburg PA
CBHW081724120626
46550CB00010B/3245